Forward

Purchasing health insurance, is a difficult, yet important decision. Everyone has different needs in regards to their healthcare. It should be noted that sometimes healthcare and health insurance are considered the same thing. We hear politicians say we need affordable healthcare. It is important to remember that healthcare is the treatment you receive from the doctor or hospital; health insurance helps you pay for that care.

Did you know that 62% of all bankruptcies are due to medical bills? The media makes it sound like these bankruptcies exist because the insurance companies are evil and deny claims or that individuals have high deductibles and co-pays. That is really not the case. First, many of the people who file bankruptcy after a medical claim had other debt to begin with and the medical bills pushed them over the limit. In that case, medical bills played a part in the bankruptcy, but are not the sole reason for the bankruptcy. Another common reason is the "intangible" expenses. These are costs associated with the claim, but not part of the claim, such as driving to and from chemotherapy or needing to get a hotel room for two nights because you are being treated at the Mayo clinic in Minnesota. Insurance does not pay for those expenses. We also have the lack of income that plays on the other side of this vicious cycle. I am self-employed, so if I have a serious medical claim, I am not working and, therefore, I am not generating any money. However, my mortgage still needs to be paid. Also, what if your spouse has to take off of work to drive you to treatment? Now you are not getting paid and neither is she. The bills still come, but the income you generate to pay them is not.

There are many ways a good insurance broker can help you avoid these pitfalls.

The Patient Protection and Affordable Care Act, passed by the Obama administration, has changed much of the insurance landscape. Many treatments that are preventive are now covered without a co-pay. The administration refers to this as "FREE PREVENTIVE CARE". I have done extensive research on this topic. As you learned when you were just a young child, there is no such thing as a free lunch. There is a cost somewhere. With the inclusion of "free preventative care", the premiums we pay have increased. I believe the cost of "free" in this case is about 12%. The more mandates we put in place, the more health insurance has to cost to cover these mandates. I use the analogy, if they mandated that all pizza had to be sold with pepperoni, you would still have to pay for the pepperoni.

There are many taxes in the Affordable Care Act (PPACA). Many of these taxes we will not feel the effect of for several years. Business owners are afraid to hire people because they fear the tax consequences. Many companies will be dropping health insurance as a benefit due to the increased cost. Some companies that have never offered benefits before are now being required to do so or pay a penalty (tax). That added expense could put them out of business or move them toward hiring independent contractors instead of employees. You have heard a lot of new terms such as insurance exchanges, mandates, subsidies and tax credits. You have heard of how money was taken from the Medicare system to pay for the PPACA.

In this book, you will learn that while the Affordable Care Act will do a lot of good things, the one thing it will not do is be affordable. You will learn how the law will add people into the system, without adding doctors. It will increase wait times to see your doctor. You might experience, at least early on, health care rationing.

As the PPACA has been in full force for over 6 months (some aspects when into effect in 2010), we are seeing smaller networks from the insurance companies as well as some insurance companies paying doctors and hospitals less per the contract. We are seeing some doctors choosing not to accept certain insurance plans due to deductibles or due to the reimbursement of particular carriers. When the law was still a bill, you heard multiple times, "if you like your insurance plan, you can keep your insurance plan" and "If you like your doctor, you can keep your doctor." We have found this not to be the case as some plans were cancelled because they did not meet the standards of the law. We also have had some doctors either drop carriers or carriers drop doctors from their network.

There are also changes to the law frequently; so many that the consumer cannot keep up with them. A good insurance broker will spend time almost daily following the changes in the law. The best advice I can give you is to always consult an experienced insurance broker. That is the best insurance policy you can have. An insurance broker works with multiple carriers so you can always find what is best for you. If you choose to work with what is called a "captive agent", meaning they only work with one carrier, you should consult more than one. You see a captive agent will be biased towards his product and often times ignorant of other products. A broker who works with several carriers will know each carrier intimately so he can advise you accordingly. The decision is too important for you to try and do it alone. I do not know enough about plumbing to try and fix the leak in my sink; I call the plumber. I do not know everything there is about tax law so my accountant does my taxes. You should do the same with your insurance. The internet is a wonderful thing, but if you are not 100% sure of what you are looking at, you should speak with an insurance professional.

When I think of insurance professionals, Butch is one of the first ones that comes to mind. I have known Butch for several years. He puts his clients first. He walks his clients through the healthcare reform requirements. How do I know? I work with him often enough on a regular basis and with his clients.

Butch is a 2014 Benefits Broker of the year finalist, and well deserving. He will take you through some of the topics of healthcare reform in this book, as he does with his own clients. He is truly a healthcare reform specialist.

If you are looking for that trusted advisor on employee benefits, Butch will definitely point you in the right direction.

To your business success,

Eric Wilson
I Sell Health, Inc.
www.isellhealth.com

The Impact of Healthcare Reform on Businesses

What every small and medium size business needs to know about health reform that will save time and money.

A Tea Party member reaches for a pamphlet titled "The Impact of Obamacare," in Littleton, N.H., in this Oct. 27, 2012, file photo.

17% of business owners surveyed say they are very familiar with the law, while 49% say they are only somewhat familiar with ObamaCare."
– Gabrielle Karol, FOXBusiness

A summary of Key Dates, New Requirement Highlights

The health care reform law - the Affordable Care Act (ACA) - Has many complex requirements for business employers and health plans. The following is a high level summary of addressing many common questions and highlighting specific components pertinent to the business.

This summary will cover the following:
- Key Dates
- The Obama Administration Delays a Major Section of Obamacare
- New Eligibility Rules
- Employer Shared Responsibility
- New Taxes
- Implications for Small Group Plans
- A Few Things Employers Need to Know for Healthcare Reform
- Inside or Outside of the Health Insurance Exchanges
- Do I Have To Buy in the Health Insurance Exchanges?
- Health Reform: Can I use My Insurance Agent?
- New Premium Models in 2014 – Rating Rules for Businesses – Families – Individuals
- Missing the Mark on Obamacare and What You Can Do to Hit The Target?
- Just Another Thing On Your Desk
- A New Approach to Employee Benefits, But in Steps

"The uncertainty caused just by the employer mandate alone can hardly be emphasized enough. It causes us to seriously hesitate before taking any risks needed to grow our businesses." Bill Feinburg, HealthReformImpacts.com and USChamber.com

Key Dates

October 1, 2013

Employers must provide all new hires and current employees with a written notice about ACA's health insurance marketplaces which are state-based or federally managed competitive marketplaces where individuals and certain businesses can purchase health insurance. In general, the notice must:

- Inform employees about the existence of the Marketplace and give a description of the services provided.
- Explain how employees may be eligible for a premium subsidy if the employee meets certain requirements.
- Inform employees that if they purchase coverage through the marketplace, they will lose any employer contribution toward the cost of their coverage, and will pay for their coverage with after tax dollars.
- Include contact information for the Marketplace and an explanation of appeal rights.
- Health plans (both fully insured and self-funded plans) must provide a Summary of Benefits and Coverage (SBC) to participants and beneficiaries. The SBC is a succinct document that provides simple and consistent information about health plan benefits and coverage in plain language. For insured plans, issuers will provide the SBC to the plan sponsor. The plan sponsor is responsible for making sure that this document is distributed to all eligible employees. For self-insured plans, the sponsor is responsible for drafting the SBC. The SBC also must be provided to newly eligible and special enrollees.

January 1, 2014

Full implementation of the healthcare law.

Employer Coverage Requirements

Employers with 50 or more full time equivalent employees will be subject to penalties if they do not provide health coverage to employees that meet levels of coverage or if the coverage they provide is not affordable. The employer mandate has been delayed to 2015 in July 2013.

The Employer Mandate -

The requirement that employers with 50 or more full-time employees or full-time equivalents (FTEs) offer health insurance to full-time employees and their dependents or pay non-tax deductible penalties.

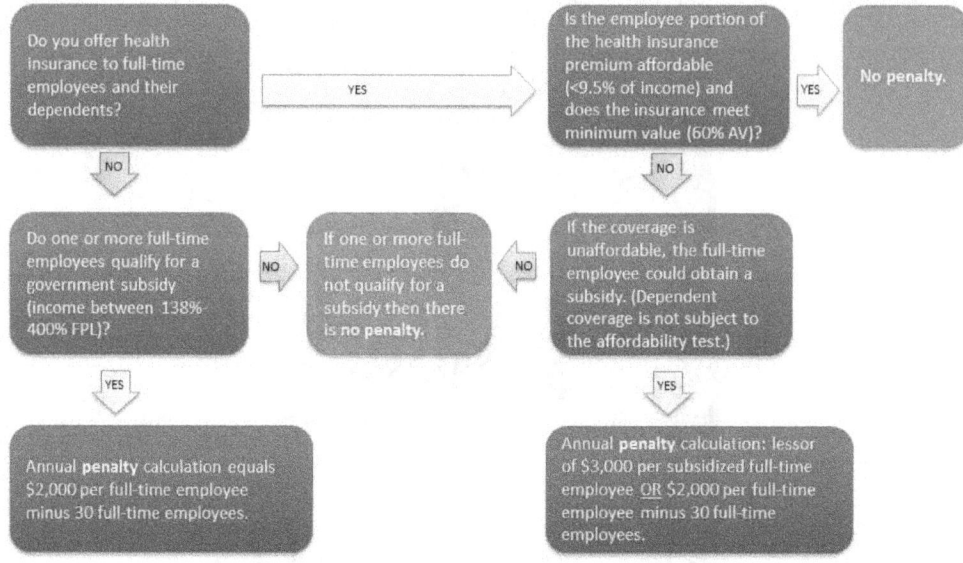

The Obama Administration Delays a Major Section of Obamacare

On July 3, 2013, the Obama Administration delayed the Employer Mandate of Obamacare until January 1, 2015. Washington claims to be listening to businesses when they were screaming that they need more time to figure out how to do their part with the new law. With only six months remaining, it is simply not enough time. This is huge for businesses in America with fifty or more employees. However, what does it mean for the future of Obamacare?

There are 200,000 businesses in the United States with fifty or more employees. Ninety-four percent of them already have health insurance in place. It is believed that even though the employer mandate will not be there for another year, most employers will not be dropping the health insurance plans. Employers are still competing for good, quality employees.

Employees are required to work at least thirty hours per week to be eligible for the health insurance. Due to the law, many businesses are not only cutting back hours, but they are laying people off to fall under this threshold of fifty employees.

With that said, some of the businesses are considering dropping the plan altogether. Let's face it, the employer 'Tax' penalty is less expensive than the group health plan. This will also allow employees, depending on their status and income, to qualify for tax subsidy that will reduce their overall premium responsibility.

Obamacare brings many questions into play. This law is so complex that after three and half years, since it was signed into law, it is still not enough time to figure out what the law actually says and to build the infrastructure. The government is trying to figure things out as they move closer. Delaying the mandate will help businesses get the answers to their questions and the Government can have additional time to figure out how to put it altogether.

Some may think this is a sign of more postponement of the healthcare law. The government has put unrealistic time frames on sections of the law. In the end, will the law stay fully intact? Time will tell... For now, buying time is what businesses needed and Washington listened.

As we move closer to healthcare reform in 2014, it is wise to stick close to experts in the field that took the time to study the trends. There are items in the law that change every week. It is difficult for the average consumer to get all the updates from the news. If the government silently announces something about the healthcare law, the media may never even pick it up and it could be very important to you.

"There's no shortage of remarkable ideas, what's missing is the will to execute them." – *Seth Godin*

"Healthcare costs are killing small businesses and sapping our economic vitality." – *SmallBusinessMajority.org*

New Eligibility Rules

Businesses are in an industry that could be vulnerable to new eligibility rules. Not only does it mandate that all employees who work, on average, 30 or more hours a week, be eligible for health insurance coverage, ACA also creates a new classification of employee called a "variable hour" employee. An employee is a variable hour employee if, at the point of hiring, it cannot be determined if the employee is a reasonably expected to work on average at least 30 hours per week. It allows an employer to defer eligibility for a period of time until it has been determined the hours that the new employee has worked.

In order to hire a new employee as a variable hour employee, employers must measure the hours these employees work for a period of time. That measurement period can be no shorter than 3 months and no longer than 12 months. Once the measurement period has been identified and the hours worked are measured, the employer can determine if the employee has met the requirement to attain eligibility. The employee will then come on to the plan (if they choose), but will continually be measured for each successive period going forward, to determine if the employee will retain eligibility.

Under ACA, certain classes of employees may be treated differently with regards to the benefits that are offered and/or the contribution that is made to these options.

Those classes are:
- Collectively bargained employees and those that are not
- Salary versus hourly employees
- By state at which a facility is maintained

Many employers are still unaware of how variable employees will impact their organization. Offering or denying benefits to this category of employee may no longer be option.

"Nearly 75 percent of manufacturers identified rising health care and insurance costs as their most important challenge. There is a strong perception that these costs will rise significantly, particularly at the small and medium-sized level." – National Association of Manufacturers, NAM.org

Employer Shared Responsibility

The ACA imposes different requirements on employers based on whether they qualify as a "large employer" or a "small employer". A large group employer employs at least 50 full-time employees, or a combination of full-time and part-time employees that exceeds 50. Small group status is defined as less than 50 full time equivalent employees.

Penalties will be imposed on large group employers who do not offer health insurance that meets minimum standards. That penalty equals $2,000 for every full time employee minus the first 30. Penalties also apply to large group employers who offer minimum insurance, but have employers who purchase their coverage through the marketplace and qualify for a subsidy. The two tests that must be met to qualify for a subsidy are: 1) The individual makes less than 400% of the federal poverty level; AND 2) The plan the employer offers is deemed unaffordable in that it exceeds 9.5% of wages earned by the employee based on the lowest cost option for the employee only coverage that is offered. The penalty in this case is $3,000 for every employee that buys coverage and qualifies for a subsidy. The gross amount of this penalty cannot exceed the total amount of the penalty for not offering insurance.

New Taxes

Comparative Effectiveness Research Tax (CER)

The Affordable Care Act (ACA) created the Patient-Centered Outcomes Research Institute (Institute) to help patients, clinicians, payers and the public make informed health decisions by advancing comparative effectiveness research. The Institute's research is to be funded, in part, by fees paid by the health insurance issuers and sponsors of self-insured health plans. These fees are widely known as Patient-Centered Outcomes Research Institute fees (PCORI fees), although they may also be called PCOR fees or Comparative effectiveness research (CER) fees.

These CER fees apply for plan years ending on or after Oct. 1, 2012 and before Oct. 1, 2019. The first possible payments will be due on July 31, 2013. For plan years ending before Oct. 1, 2013, the fee is $1 per covered life under the plan. For plan years ending on or after Oct. 1, 2013, and before Oct. 1, 2014, the fee increases to $2 per covered life. For plan years ending on or after Oct 1, 2014, the fee amount will grow based on increases in the projected per capita amount of National Health Expenditures.

Reinsurance Tax

ACA established a risk-spreading program, called the transitional reinsurance program, to help stabilize premiums for coverage in the individual market during the first three years of Exchange operation (2014 through 2016) when individuals with higher-cost medical needs gain insurance coverage. ACA requires health insurance issuers and plan sponsors of self-insured group health plans to pay fees to support the reinsurance program. For 2014, HHS proposed a national contribution rate of $63 per year. An issuer's or plan sponsor's reinsurance fee would be calculated by multiplying the average number of covered lives (employees and their dependents) during the benefit year for all of the entity's plans and coverage that must pay contributions, by the national contribution rate for the benefit year.

Health Industry Tax

The health insurance provider's fee applies to all "covered entities," defined as any entity that provides health insurance for any United States health risk. The fee will be assessed on health insurers' premium revenue above $25 million. Beginning in 2019, the cost of the fee will increase based on the rate of premium growth. This fee will not apply to plans that are self-funded.

Cadillac Tax

For taxable years beginning in 2018, ACA imposes a 40 percent excise tax on high-cost group health coverage. The Cadillac tax provision taxes the amount, if any, by which the monthly cost of an employee's applicable employer [sponsored health coverage exceeds the annual limitation ($10,200 annualized single premium and $27,500 annualized family premium).

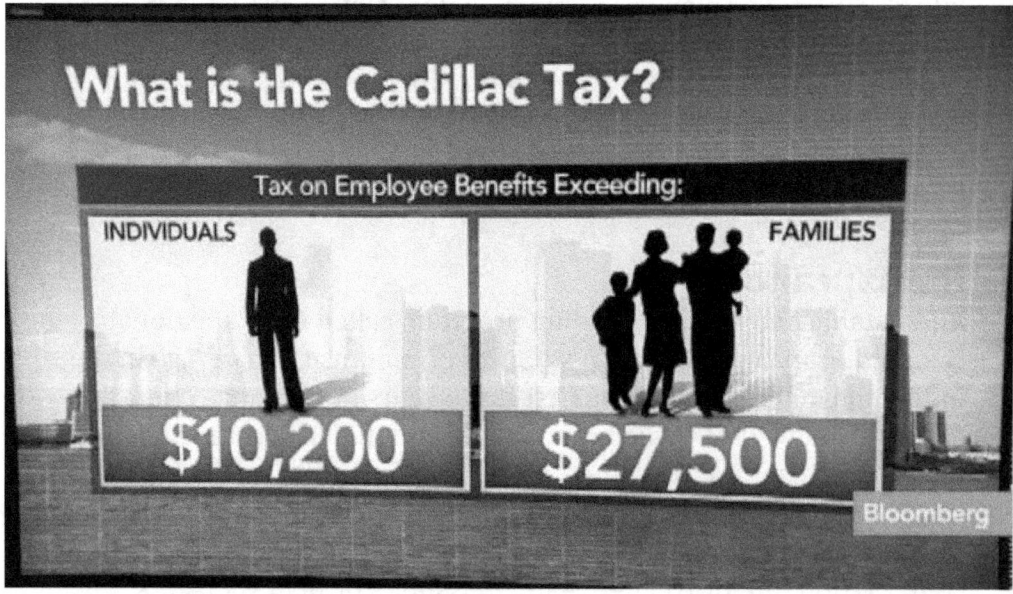

Photo Source: BusinessWeek.com

Implications for Small Group Plans

Effective for plan years beginning on or after Jan. 1, 2014, health insurance issuers in the small group market will be generally prohibited from determining premium rates based on health status. Issuers will be able to vary premium rates based only on age, rating area, sex, and tobacco use. This reform, which is often referred to as "community rating", does not apply to grandfather plans nor does it apply to large group plans.

Additionally, rates for these plans will no longer be offered on a composite basis, but instead a different premium will apply for every individual on the plan. - a mechanism called "List Bill".

Pay or Play Decision

In 2014, employers with more than 50 employees are required to offer minimal essential health coverage to employees or be subject to a penalty. In an employer survey conducted in early 2013, there are indications that many employers will "play" and continue to offer health coverage to their employees. This provision has been delayed to 2015.

A Few Things Businesses Need to Know for Healthcare Reform

It is important for employers to know where to begin in the months and years ahead with healthcare reform. Focusing on the right things for your business and your employees is essential in healthcare coverage. It may involve changing the processes as well as updating documents and materials to comply with the new law.

Many of the components of the healthcare law are beginning to unfold. When they signed it into law, they only signed a concept. The rulings and how things will actually work are still being determined by the federal government as we move along. Some people believe this gave the government the opportunity to bypass the steps needed to make other portions become a law. This is a nice way to get their way without asking for permission.

The number of employees will determine what action or actions you will need to take. The law uses a magic number of 50 employees as a bench mark. If the company has 49 or less, many of the laws do not apply to them. If you are 50 or more, there are more requirements that are required for those businesses.

The government did get smart with this benchmark of 50 employees. They are using what they call "Full-time equivalent" employees. They take the number of hours worked by all of the part-time employees and divide by 120 hours. This will give you a total for "Full-time equivalent" employees and is added to the full-time employee numbers.

For groups filing 250 or more W-2 forms are required to report the cost of employee's health insurance coverage on the employees. At this time, this reporting is only informational for the employee and will not have to pay any taxes on this benefit. Some employees will be in shock and will treat their job with more respect. Others will not care and take advantage of the system even more.

A tax credit is a perk for businesses and will help them with their employee benefits. The Small Business Health Care Tax Credit was put in the law to encourage business owners and tax-exempt organizations to offer health insurance coverage for their employees. Some businesses will not think this is enough incentive. For those business owners on the fence in providing benefits, or already do, this is icing on the cake. In 2014, the tax credit will be only available through the Small Business Health Options Program (SHOP). At the time of this writing, a portion of the SHOP has been delayed.

A number of taxes and fees related to the healthcare law will change the game plan for employers. Some of them will have a dramatic impact on the group's premiums. Having an idea on where the fees are going to and effective dates will allow you to make business planning a little easier.

Health Insurance Exchanges, or Marketplace, could change how businesses cover their employees in the future. As an employer, you are required to provide all employees with information about the Exchanges. This will include the employee eligibility to participate in the Exchanges and the health insurance subsidies if the group coverage provided by the employer is considered unaffordable by the Affordable Care Act's guidelines.

Business owners and employees are not required to buy inside the Exchanges. There may be some perks, but some of those perks may not be eligible for the business. Buying outside of the exchange may be a more viable option for businesses. Businesses will be required to implement changes within the plans they offer. The coverage changes will be based on benefit expansion or coverage limits. These changes will affect groups small and large. Your current carrier will inform you of these changes.

The out-of-pocket limits on the plan cannot exceed the limit as outlined by the Health Savings Accounts (HSAs). Those of you that have an HSA currently, this may be no news for you.

Essential Health Benefits and Minimum Essential Coverage is a key part of the expansion. These are benefits like maternity, preventative medicine coverage, etc. This could be a good or bad thing for the group. Although the plan will have more benefit, the premium will reflect the cost of the coverage.

All in all, when you add more 'benefit' to a plan, the cost of that plan could only go up. There are some good things that came out of this law, but not everything. Businesses have to watch where their dollars are going with the new healthcare law. They are not required to be experts on the law, but stay informed. Having basic knowledge will help you move forward in the years ahead for providing employee benefits for the company.

Inside or Outside of the Health Insurance Exchanges

Businesses, individuals and families are even more confused about where they can buy health insurance come 2014. Some think they have to buy inside the exchange. This is simply not the case. So what do you do? Get informed!

The exchanges were designed to offer a richer set of plans than most people in America are used to through their employer. The government knew this going into it. On top of that, they created an incentive to use the exchange through subsidies for those who qualify, but only within the exchange. The family size and income will play a major role on what and how much subsidy you will qualify for from the government inside the exchange. There are no government subsidies outside of the exchange.

Inside the exchange, there will be a Gold, Silver, Bronze and a Platinum plans. The insurance carriers who offer plans inside the exchange will not be required to offer all four plans. They are required to offer one gold and one silver plan. Each plan will have slightly different essential benefits.

There is no ruling on what will be available outside of the exchange, at the time of this writing. The understanding is there will be more flexibility in choosing a plan that meets your needs versus what is available inside the exchange. As of now, the non-grandfathered plans will include more of the essential benefits that are required by the law. This could be a plan you currently have right now. An example of essential benefits is maternity coverage. The maternity benefit will be added to your plan, along with the associated costs, as well as new plans starting January 2014.

This can be a good or bad thing, depending... It is bad for that single 30 year-old male entrepreneur that is unmarried. He will be paying for a benefit that he will not be able to use unless he gets married and they are having children. The flip side is a growing family does not have to wait a period of time until maternity kicks in. This will eventually have an impact on the premiums. But, what won't?

The plans outside of the exchange will have more flexibility for plan selections. If you want that $5,000 deductible, because you are willing to take the risk to offset premiums, you can have it. If you want to keep your HSA plan, you can. You can at least at the time of this writing.

Having this flexibility will allow premiums to go down. There is talk going around the small and medium size business industry that the plans within the exchanges will cost you more than outside the exchange. This will give many the advantage of buying outside the exchanges at a much lower cost. Especially, when you make more than the income required to qualify for the subsidy by the government.

Make sure you know your choices going into 2014. The media and your friends do not work in the industry and they could only provide one-sided information. Be informed for 2014.

Do I Have To Buy in the Health Insurance Exchanges?

Healthcare reform is moving at full throttle to be ready for January 1st, 2014. Some people did not even know that healthcare reform was signed into law by the current Administration. Most people are still confused on how things will pan out. The health insurance exchanges are going to be real, but you need to know your options before pulling the trigger.

The media and your next door neighbor are doing a good job with informing you on what is in store for healthcare reform in 2014. Some are saying you have to buy inside the health insurance exchanges, but they do not know why. So, why do you have to buy inside the health insurance exchanges? Ask them, and they will not know.

For small businesses, a portion of the S.H.O.P. has been delayed and will not be ready in time for 2014. However, for individuals and families that work for companies that do not offer health insurance, they can easily go to the health insurance exchanges starting as early as October 1, 2013 with an effective date of January 1st, 2014. Choosing to go to the exchanges, you may qualify for the tax subsidy for your premiums and out-of-pocket expenses. Of course, not everyone will qualify for this. The tax subsidy takes in account family filing status, income and a few other factors. If you qualify for the subsidy, this can be good for your pocket-book. Many professionals and families that do a little better, income wise, may not qualify for the subsidies. If you do not qualify for subsidy, then there is no added value for using the exchanges, none.

Buying outside the exchange will give you more options versus what is available inside the exchange. The plan options will be more flexible and allows you to have more control over your health plan coverage. This can help you manage your personal interests as well as your budget. For those people looking for more choices on their healthcare coverage, this can be a good thing.

Inside the exchange, you will only be looking at five different plan levels from each carrier. The only difference between the carriers is the monthly premium, as long as you are comparing the same plan. It is pretty cookie cutter, to say the least. You are limited to those options and that's it.

Review plans outside the exchanges with a health insurance broker can be very advantageous for you and your business. The flexibility of plans and pricing options will empower you. Now you can turn off the news and stop listening to your neighbor. You are in control versus the subject of what the government dictating to be bought inside the exchanges.

"Businesses, individuals and families are even more confused about where they can buy health insurance come 2014. Get Informed!"

"The previously passed Affordable Care Act will only impose large tax increases and burdensome regulations." - NAM.org

Health Reform: Can I use My Insurance Agent?

It is full speed ahead with questions about how healthcare reform will pan out come later this year, 2013. Open enrollment starts October first. What does that mean for you? It means a lot of confusion and unanswered questions. This is where your insurance agent comes in.

The agents have a huge role in the lives of individuals, families and businesses. They depend on these insurance agents for their expertise, advice and to be there when they need them the most. Many people and businesses need the guidance in making the right choices when it comes to their insurance. They do not want to be the expert. They have enough problems and personal goals going on in their own lives, to have to worry about insurance coverage. This is why they work with a trusted insurance agent.

Health insurance has become more of a commodity these days, but people still do not understand what they have. The confusion has created such a crisis in America. Many people do not know what they have for their insurance coverage. Insurance agents are there to work on the behalf of the policyholders and to recommend the best coverage for their situation, for the money.

Healthcare reform, or Obamacare, has really taken people's minds for a spin. Some people think they can only buy through the health

insurance exchanges come 2014. This is simply not the case.
The media takes a small little piece of information and twists it. Then they twist it again. What are the facts? Will anyone ever know?

Of course we can, with the right resources. The media does not have the incentive to study the books, read the trade articles, go to meetings and invest hours in knowing the health insurance arena. The healthcare bill was over 2,000 pages and more insurance agents have read the bill than congress and the media combined.

There are not any facts on this. However, agents have a vested interest in knowing their industry. The media only needs a teaser that sells.

Health insurance agents will play a major role with healthcare reform. It has been made public by congress that the agents will participate inside the exchanges come 2014. This is important for people, because they still get the expertise and guidance of experts in the field. This gives individuals, families and business owners a piece of mind when it comes to their health insurance and employee benefits going forward.
Even if someone wants nothing to do with the exchanges, they can purchase a plan outside of the exchange. Agents will have a role in this part as well. It's business as usual there.

Despite the commission being squashed again and again, the agents are studying the reform and getting ready for the change. There is no reason why you cannot continue to use your insurance agent in the future as it all unfolds before us.

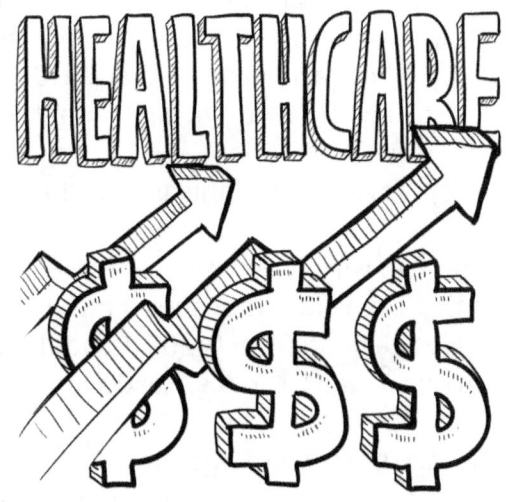

New Premium Models in 2014 – Rating Rules for Businesses – Families – Individuals

New rating factors for businesses, as well as individuals and families, will play a key part in planning for 2014. Some businesses will be smacked with a 50+ percent increase based on some characteristics that are at play with the new rating rules. With that said, some businesses will be excited to know their premiums are slated to lower. There are some key items you need to know that go into the new rating model called Community Rating.

There are a lot of questions that come up regarding the healthcare law. Some think it will be for free. In some cases, it will be pretty close to free. Others will find out real soon when their premiums change, they may possibly go down, but for the most part they will go up due to changes in the Affordable Care Act.

Rates can vary based on if the plan covers an individual or a family. Health Insurance companies must utilize a per member rating process. The insurance company adds up the rate for each family member to arrive at the family premium. Rates for only the three oldest family members under age 21 will be taken into account in addition to the rates for those over 21.

A State may establish up to seven rating areas under the proposed ruling. The rating areas must meet one of the following:
1) There are no more than seven areas based on county, three-digit ZIP codes or metropolitan/non-metropolitan statistical areas.
2) There is only one area in the state.

Rates can vary based on age. They cannot vary more than 3 to 1 for adults. The rule establishes a uniform age band. A child age band is: A single age band from 0-20. An adult age band is: A one year age band starting at age 21 to 63. Lastly, a single age band is for 64 and older.

Tobacco users were not left out of the equation. Insurance carriers can charge higher rates for people who use tobacco products. They are also limited on what they can charge. Rates for people who use tobacco products cannot vary by more than 1.5 times the rate of the non-tobacco user.

The premiums could have a toll one way or the other come 2014, depending on the variables in the census of the employer group and the new rating rules. The business may or may not have control on the ratings however, you can start planning your strategy for 2014 and beyond. Making some adjustments now could off-set costs come next year. If you do not do anything, or the current agent or broker does not do anything, you could be suffering with the 50 + percent increase putting a huge burden on the cash-flow of the business. Cash-flow is so crucial for the survival of a business.

Missing the Mark on Obamacare and What You Can Do to Hit the Target

The healthcare law imposed 82 deadlines onto the Obama Administration. They missed exactly half of all the deadlines in three years. Does this mean it will fail?
The Obama Administration has already delayed several key components of the law. They still believe the health insurance exchange, or known as marketplace, will be ready on time. Although, somewhere it says the deadline is September 30th, the day before it opens. This does not give much time for any further delays, quirks or any personality conflicts.

Some are even saying that the Administration is picking and choosing what they want to devote their energies to and what they won't, based on political agenda. The original intent is falling apart. Unbroken promises?

The law has a lot of good things in it. The unfortunate thing is the law was filled with mostly garbage, unbroken promises and sky rocketing premiums due to more mandates. Each mandates cost the insurance company money. Just like anything else, a company will pass the extra costs back on to the consumer.

The government has definitely missed the mark at the taxpayer's expense. But, what do they care? The politicians themselves are exempt from the healthcare law. As a business owner, executive, HR director, or employee, how are you supposed to keep up with the changes and stay focused on your day-to-day operations? Here are a few things you can do:

Study the law (not what the media tells you). This is very time-consuming and will take you away from your daily activities.

Keep in touch with your insurance agent/broker and/or health reform consultant. This is key as you move closer to making decisions on what your health insurance going forward.

If your insurance agent is not available, not responding, or seems unclear about things... Look for a new insurance agent. There are many that are up to speed on what's going on.

Call your insurance carrier directly. They will provide you with some information about changes. Again, this option is not as great as working with an insurance agent that has been keeping up with the trends. They will just overwhelm you with information and it's up to you to figure it out.

Rinse and Recycle

It should be clear that you would need to consult an insurance agent or consultant on healthcare reform. Hitting your target for employee benefits with the new law still takes some planning. Even if you are a tiny business with just a few employees, you still need to strategize your approach heading into 2014.

Of course, you can shoot a shotgun at a target without ever shooting a gun before. You could hit the target with a little of beginners luck. However, now do it in a crowded room. Try pulling the trigger to hit the target. Not so easy, is it? That crowded room is filled with people that are dependent on you to make the right decisions. This room is filled with your family, your business, your employees, and your peers. You need to have resources and expertise in order to make more accurate decisions heading into 2014. Otherwise, your target could be missed.

Just Another Thing On Your Desk

Everyone has tasks to do on their desk and will always run into issues of completing more. Some things just have to come off the employer's desk. This is where outsourcing or delegation is needed. For some small employers, it is hard to give up control of some things, or even know where to start. Employee benefits is a key item to retain employees, but where do you find the time to keep up with all the compliance changes? The fines could be devastating to the bottom line.

A small manufacturer with about 23 employees in the south suburbs of Chicago felt they had control over their employee benefits. For several years, all they did was contact the insurance company directly and, of course, the insurance company was glad to skip the insurance broker and take the business. Note: The premiums are the same either way.

As the employee benefits arena changed with healthcare reform, the employer felt they were not receiving the right facts and information needed moving forward. The insurance companies were being bias with their comparisons and it was starting to get harder and harder to find the right information for their business.
Even the information they have, took large amounts of time. By delegating to their assistant, it still cost money and time. It is now just another thing on their desk to work with year after year. By adding the complex changes to the mix with the new law, it increases this time at least two-fold.

This happens everyday with manufacturers and small businesses. Employers are having a hard time with the changes and are looking for ways to get it off their desk.

Employee benefits is a real key item in employee retention. It is a sought-out benefit from talented employees looking for employment or to advance their career. It is an investment that an employer has to make in order grow and be profitable.

Employers do not have time to add anything else to their list of items. It needs to be taken care of but where do they find someone who is qualified and has the time?

There are advisors and consultants that have resources and tools at their fingertips because they work with employers on a regular basis. Besides staying up to speed with plan design changes from insurance company to insurance company, the resources help keep employers compliant. Employers may start seeing more and more Department of Labor and ERISA audits. The government is hiring more auditors to increase the number of audits; fines. This can impose hefty fines for employers and will cost them more than the investment of an advisor or consultant and the requirements in order to be compliant.
By keeping this item on your desk, how would you know if you are compliant? You have a business to run and to keep growing market share. It is time to take the employee benefits and compliance issues off your desk and put on someone else's desk. It is an investment in the growth of the company.

A New Approach to Employee Benefits, But in Steps

Some employers have been with the same insurance agent for years. The employers are either complacent and really trust their insurance broker or consultant, or they do not want to "rock the boat" on the relationship. This could create a problem for the employer.

If the employer gets in a jam with being non-compliant, they can always fire the insurance broker/consultant, but the employer still has a problem to fix. How about fixing the problem before it occurs?

The first thing employers need to do is make their current insurance broker or consultant accountable. Their "easy ride" could cost you, the employer, a lot of money. This could be big fines or over paying premiums or commissions/fees to the broker. None of which an employer wants or needs to operate their business.

Health care reform has change the game for employers. Providing benefits is only a piece of it. Often insurance brokers will use the employee benefits 'fluff' to cover up their lack of understand of the new law. With the new law, compliance has become a huge issue for employers.

Even very small employers have a much higher chance of being on the radar than ever before.

Some insurance brokers will stay clear of helping employers in this arena. Employers need to find an insurance broker or consultant that has the resources to keep employers compliant.

Insurance Brokers or consultants that come up with a new approach to employee benefits will lay things out in steps. The employer can take small steps to become compliant in addition to adding value with employee benefits.

It is a great approach for employers that do not know where to start. You do not normally eat a delicious apple pie all at once. You take a bite and savor the moment. Taking a "bite" in benefits compliance can savor the moment of not paying additional penalties that could have been avoided.

If this conversation has not occurred with your current insurance broker or consultant, you should add a step to the process by firing them. The second step to add is find a way to become compliant with someone who is resourceful. Many insurance brokers and consultants have them; you just have to find them. They are out there.

Compliance is the real deal. With the new health care law, it will become more important for an employer to make sure they have their ducks in a row. If you, the employer, loses an audit, it is money out of your pocket that could have gone to more useful things. Get your new approach to employee benefits, but in steps.

About the Author

Butch Zemar is a scuba diving extraordinaire, Healthcare Reform Specialist and a 2014 Benefits Selling's Broker of the Year Finalist. Butch also has published an e-book on Healthcare Reform to help small to mid-size companies stay ahead of their industry trends in the amid of changes in the healthcare law.

After serving in the Navy for four years achieving an E-5 (AW) class, working in Naval Aviation Electronics, Zemar left the military and began a career in scuba diving. As a deep shipwreck explorer and instructor, he began training divers in the Virginia Beach, VA, area in 2001.

For the past 20 years, Butch has been involved in all aspects of diving – and continues to see the world by diving in the oceans, the Great Lakes and Midwest quarries.

After being involved in small business retail sales, Zemar was drawn to the insurance and financial arena. In 2004, Zemar established an independent insurance agency near Chicago, offering a full spectrum of health insurance and asset protection products. The agency now offers all lines of insurance to their business clients.

As President of Elite Benefits of America, Zemar leads a team of professionals committed to providing the highest in product offerings and long-term service and support. He has established a reputation as a "health care reform specialist" with a deep understanding of the industry and provides businesses with comprehensive benefit solutions throughout persistent healthcare reform.

Zemar is actively developing informative resources, such as articles and videos, that deliver vital information on healthcare reform and employer options. Elite Benefits of America has consultative packages for employers, as well as insurance solutions, to keep employers compliant with healthcare reform and keep skyrocketing premiums under control.

Elite Benefits of America Insurance Services - Specializing in Business Insurance, Risk Management and Employee Benefits for Small and Medium Size Businesses.

Elite Benefits of America has variety of products and services that cater to small and medium size business owners. Our objective is to assist companies in lowering their overall costs of their risk, in addition to helping them attract and retain the best employees to work with their company. Elite Benefits of America covers basic insurance procurement to advance consultation and implementation of specialized services. Elite Benefits of America delivers superior solutions on all lines, including business insurance, risk management and employee's benefits.

For more information about Elite Benefits of America, visit us online at www.EliteBenefits.net or call 888-535-3006.

The Elite Benefits of America accepts no liability or responsibility to any person or organization as a consequence of any reliance upon the information contained in this book. Every effort is made to provide information that is true and accurate. However, information contained in this book are subject to change at any time. Health care reform is based on the Patient Protection and Affordable Care Act of 2010 and is subject to change by federal and local governments. Elite Benefits of America has no control or influence on political parties or regulations. The information in this book should not be considered legal, financial or other advice and is not intended to replace consultation with a qualified professional or specific written confirmation from Elite Benefits of America. Please seek an adviser in the area needed for you and your business.

NOTES

NOTES

NOTES

NOTES